D1370129

Funding for this book provided by:

Union Smart Start
a partnership for children

Just the Opposite
Fast / Slow

Exactamente lo opuesto
Rápido / Lento

Sharon Gordon

 **Marshall Cavendish**
Benchmark
New York

This car is fast.

❖

Este carro es rápido.

This car is slow.

❖

Este carro es lento.

This bus is fast.

---❖---

Este autobús es rápido.

This bus is slow.

❖

Este autobús es lento.

This truck is fast.

❖

Este camión es rápido.

This truck is slow.

❖

Este camión es lento.

This bike is fast.

❖

Esta bicicleta es rápida.

This bike is slow.

❖

Esta bicicleta es lenta.

This boat is fast.

❖

Este bote es rápido.

This boat is slow.

❖

Este bote es lento.

This horse is fast.

Este caballo es rápido.

This horse is slow.

---❖---

Este caballo es lento.

This train is fast.

❖

Este tren es rápido.

This train is slow.

❖

Este tren es lento.

This airplane is fast.

❖

Este avión es rápido.

This airplane is slow.

❖

Este avión es lento.

My skates are fast.

Mis patines son rápidos.

Go slow!

❖

¡Ve lentamente!

Words We Know
Palabras que sabemos

airplane
avión

bike
bicicleta

boat
bote

bus
autobús

car
carro

horse
caballo

stakes
patines

train
tren

truck
camión

Index

Índice

About the Author
Datos biográficos de la autora

Sharon Gordon has written many books for young children. She has always worked as an editor. Sharon and her husband Bruce have three children, Douglas, Katie, and Laura, and one spoiled pooch, Samantha. They live in Midland Park, New Jersey.

❖

Sharon Gordon ha escrito muchos libros para niños. Siempre ha trabajado como editora. Sharon y su esposo Bruce tienen tres niños, Douglas, Katie y Laura, y una perra consentida, Samantha. Viven en Midland Park, Nueva Jersey.

With thanks to Nanci Vargus, Ed.D. and Beth Walker Gambro, reading consultants

Marshall Cavendish Benchmark
99 White Plains Road
Tarrytown, New York 10591-9001
www.marshallcavendish.us

Library of Congress Cataloging-in-Publication Data

Gordon, Sharon.
[Fast slow. Spanish & English]
Fast slow = Rápido lento / Sharon Gordon. — Bilingual ed.
p. cm. — (Bookworms. Just the opposite)
Includes index.
ISBN-13: 978-0-7614-2447-5 (bilingual ed.)
ISBN-10: 0-7614-2447-4 (bilingual ed.)
ISBN-13: 978-0-7614-2367-6 (Spanish ed.)
ISBN-10: 0-7614-1570-X (English ed.)
1. Speed—Juvenile literature. 2. Polarity—Juvenile literature. 3. Vehicles—Juvenile literature.
4. English language—Synonyms and antonyms—Juvenile literature. I. Title. II. Title: Rápido lento.
III. Series: Gordon, Sharon. Bookworms. Just the opposite (Spanish & English)

QC137.5.G6718 2007
531'.112—dc22
2006017274

Spanish Translation and Text Composition by Victory Productions, Inc.
www.victoryprd.com

Photo Research by Anne Burns Images

Cover Photos: *Corbis*: (top-Forest Johnson), (bottom-Ariel Skelley)

The photographs in this book are used with permission and through the courtesy of: *Corbis*: pp. 1 (left), 12 Kevin R. Morris; p. 3 Jennie Woodcock Reflections Photo Library; p. 4 Thomas Ropke; pp. 5, 16, 20 (top left) (bottom right) *Corbis*; p. 6 J. Barry O'Rourke; pp. 7, 21 (bottom right) Alan Schein; pp. 10, 20 (bottom left) Forest Johnson; p. 11 Ariel Skelley; pp. 14, 21 (bottom left) Georgina Bowater; p. 15 Louise Gubb; pp. 18, 21 (top right) Norbert Schaefer; p. 19 Paul Barton; *Photri*: pp. 1 title page (right), 13, 17, 21 (top middle); pp. 2, 21 (top left) Ken Kaminsky; pp. 8, 20 (top right) Mark E. Gibson; p. 9 Fotopic.

Series design by Becky Terhune

Printed in Malaysia
1   3   5   6   4   2